If the Darkness Is Lacking

If the Darkness Is Lacking

Poems by

Meggie Royer

© 2023 Meggie Royer. All rights reserved.
This material may not be reproduced in any form, published,
reprinted, recorded, performed, broadcast,
rewritten or redistributed without
the explicit permission of Meggie Royer.
All such actions are strictly prohibited by law.

Cover design by Shay Culligan
Cover image by Will (cashoyboy)
Author photo by the author

ISBN: 978-1-63980-441-2

Kelsay Books
502 South 1040 East, A-119
American Fork, Utah 84003
Kelsaybooks.com

Acknowledgments

Sincere thanks to the editors of the following publications in which several poems first appeared:

The Hamilton Stone Review: "Aubade for My Doppelganger"

The New Social Worker: "Impostor Syndrome"

Qua Literary and Fine Arts Magazine: "Thanatophobia," "Non-Sonnet for Women Who Don't Want to Be Mothers"

Slippery Elm: "True Crime"

WhimsicalPoet: "Living Will"

Thank you to every reader old and new, and all the English teachers along the way.

Thank you to all the women who work tirelessly every day to create a better world.

About the Book

If the Darkness Is Lacking is inspired by Royer's fear of mortality, her fascination with memory and true crime, and her personal, near decade-long involvement with the field of domestic violence, an endeavor that often encompasses all of the above.

She has alternately worked as a hospital-based advocate, a shelter education coordinator, an academic researcher on sexual assault, and as a preventionist at a statewide domestic violence coalition. For several years, she and her colleague were two of only a handful of people in Minnesota tracking, monitoring, and analyzing annual intimate partner homicides in the state.

If the Darkness Is Lacking is a culmination of the life-altering assault Royer experienced as a teenager, a desire to pay homage to all the women taken far too soon, and the inseparable, agonizing task of realizing that one can never return to childhood.

Contents

I. Misogyny

Lunar Cycle	15
Aubade for My Doppelganger	16
Teaching Your Daughter How Not to Walk Alone at Night	17
Exorcism	18
One in Three	19
Impostor Syndrome	20
Witness Impact Statement	21
Night Terror	22
Hypothermia	23

II. Missingness

Paranormal Activity	27
The Charley Project	28
True Crime	29
Twin Flame	30
Plate Tectonics	31
A Group of Grows Is Called a Murder	32
The Doppler Effect	33
The Final Girl	34

III. Memory

Ode to Petrichor	37
Post-Apocalypse	38
Elegy to Quarter-Life Crisis	39
Dissertation on Nostalgia	40
The New Year	41
Climate Change	42
Aesop's Fables	43
The Patron Saint of Leaving the Past in the Past	44

IV. Melancholia

Theories of Loneliness   47
Ode to the Worst Day of Your Life   48
Twelve Steps   49
Metonymy   50

V. Milestones

Something Borrowed, Something Blue   53
Lessons on Preparing for an Ending   54
Love Poem to Early Twenties   55
Thanatophobia   56
Folie à Deux   57
Chrysalis   58
Non-Sonnet for Women Who Don't Want to Be
    Mothers   59
Living Will   60

I. Misogyny

Lunar Cycle

Upon the eve of every full moon, the women would come
to the water's edge, would fill the shallow bowls with salt,
& empty their dresses of every living thing—seaweed,
marsh, red milk snakes coiled like a hangman's rope.
And there was nothing but dozens of women
for miles, across every shoreline, in every boat,
along every stream. For awhile, just for one night,
they outnumbered the men. And each one had a story to tell—
being hunted, or being stolen,
or having gone missing. Or being carried, screaming,
to the back of a truck bed. Some held down, others tied.
The moon would turn. It would pink. It would purple.
And when it reached its peak, when the dresses were emptied,
they took the chosen man from the village,
& dragged him to the river,
& sent him away, & his mouth was filled with stones,
And he knew, then, at last, what it was like to be a woman,
howling without any sound.

Aubade for My Doppelganger

Have you regained your faith in mirrors?
Was it easy for you to be lost at first?
Are you the knife, the raven, or the thorn?
If you can, write a song for your held tongue,
for your stolen sleep. The winters will be hard.
One morning, a clot could pass through you like a storm,
hair spilling down your back like leaves.
I know you.
You have measured the dark
and found it lacking.
You are not any closer to feeling found.
There are still men left to forgive.
In dreams, the village healer beads a necklace of serotonin;
you swallow as many as you can.
Every new moon an untaught alchemy,
pines raising over the mountains like bone.

Teaching Your Daughter How Not to Walk Alone at Night

In your hometown, they found the body of a young woman
on a golf course in the early morning,
dawn verdant like a storm.
When asked why, the suspect said he didn't know.
But truly not knowing
is not knowing how short the duration
of the rest of your life will be, or if lucky, how long—
how many mangoes ahead of you to unpeel,
how many songs to sing, how many decades of loss
to unlearn. As if, in passing,
you don't fear for your safety every day.
The way a new house goes to ground,
floorboards pitted with salt,
like waking in the middle of the night for water
& missing a step on the landing,
body filled, at last,
with air.

Exorcism

Somehow, the beehives were lit on fire over the summer,
queens coiled like dark medallions in the brush.
Loss, when it arrives, marks its territory like a wolf.
Here, a woman dies every other week.
Once, one was backed over
by a pickup truck, her daughter watching
as finches swarmed in the dusk.
Easy to write & hard to name—how a calf
was pulled from inside its mother at the same time,
body slick with red, hungry for milk.
There were leafcutters that night
& they dove through the sky like stars,
one child falling,
the other rising.

One in Three

In some woods, a man bends, praying,
koi rising from the water like steam.
Another ghost crossing the threshold,
twilight still laced against its skull.
How to describe the moment a person ceases
to be a person, or how to shape the words,
how to find your way back up from on your knees.
Something must be given
if something else is taken away.
Phase change—the transition of one state of matter
to another.
Like the moon cut into a window,
like being born over and over again
& still not getting the hang
of not dying.

Impostor Syndrome

At some point, the moon was assembled
with the intention of surpassing human knowledge—
molten, unremitting,
arc of construction paper against the sky.
In Utah, a man shot his girlfriend just because he could.
No backstory, no preceding history
of which anyone was aware.
No wonder the parameters of human myth
are so unbounded;
no wonder we think we know someone
we never knew at all.
How ardently you can be afraid—
the moon could be a planet, inhabited,
flush with our worst fears of who might reside there,
or just another glow transmitting into the dark,
like the deep, momentary terror
of a man slowing his car beside you
only to realize he's arrived at home.

Witness Impact Statement

Every so often,
a twin will mistake themselves for the other.
Not fright exactly,
but the same uncanny feeling
of forgetting what you entered a room for.
It could be nothing
or something twice doubled.
Once, a man asked every customer at a bank
to lie down on the floor and wait
then left the establishment.
That's how you cause motion sickness.
That's how you make one thing
look like another.
A red vase, flush against a window,
could be a heart. A spoon could be a fish,
scales exposed like electrical wires.
Once, a man shot a woman
because he thought she was his girlfriend.
It wasn't a bullet. It couldn't be.
It was a pearl poised, so improbably,
on the cusp of the equinox.

Night Terror

Once, a neighbor arrived in the early hours
believing she'd woken to a man in her room.
What the mind conjures in sleep, it fears in day,
minutes like stones
pressed into the path of an echo.
What stills the body
could be neurons breaking like waves,
or stepping from a dream like a robe.
He was never there, but he was.
Not the scent of him, but the shape.
When it was over, the memory
lasted longer than the image,
caught like a fish
in the mouth of the only bear
that ever loved it.

Hypothermia

The bodies of hibernating animals
are too cold to procedure electrical currents
that result in dreaming.
If they could, a thousand nights of blue,
lichen against every rock like sugar.
Once, while she was sleeping
a man took the life of his girlfriend.
No violence before that. No signs.
If nature works as it should,
the dream she was having
was a good one. At least there was that.
Not every thing we do to each other has a name.
Sometimes, it's best left alone,
buried too deep
to emerge when winter ends.

II. Missingness

Paranormal Activity

Sometimes, a demon is the best excuse
to do the worst things to each other
we'd already do anyway.
Not all demises
are untimely.
Not all animals pretend not to speak.
A premonition isn't a portent;
it's a bird learning another language.
Most hauntings don't begin at home;
they start in the ground before it was built.
Every once in awhile,
the life that flashes before your eyes
is just an echo of your death looking backward.
It might spill across a shadow like fire,
or empty a reflection from a mirror.
It might be the last time we see each other alive,
cameras off, windows open,
moon dipped into the lake like fondue.

The Charley Project

Is the most detailed online database of missing persons cases.

Ambiguous loss, or, sometimes what leaves
doesn't want to be found.
If you place one shoe with the next,
sometimes they both turn the same direction.
If you filter by year, you also filter by grief.
Occasionally, a child will pretend to be another child
if it means living like a child.
This isn't to say being brought into the world
is a sequel.
It's to say that on the web, a photo can be anyone
you need it to be.
Another year, another quiet alchemy transformed.
Another sea bordering the snow.
If they're online, they're alive—
one river bounded to the one below it,
one timezone folded neatly
into the next.

True Crime

Is the term for the dawn purpling and giving itself back
to the sky, or, an obsession with the space
between missing & misunderstanding,
which is the same width
as the space between startling
& starting again.
Sometimes, it's enough to believe people willingly disappear,
that somewhere they move around in the world
like fog pulled from breath in the cold,
that you can begin again, & again, & again,
until you find a life that suits you,
and sometimes, it's too much to know
a person gone missing
can choose not to be found.
Not the way you wake blindly in the dark
forgetting where you are,
but the way a coast guard's beacon
pierces through the night like a storm,
not really searching for anything
but its own reflection.

Twin Flame

In the local coffee shop, a girl who resembles Claire
from *Six Feet Under.*
How easily everything can look like something else.
In the romantic science fiction film *I Origins,*
a deceased woman's eyes later found—metaphorically—
in a small child's.
Irises the same, down to the color & size.
Some mornings, you wake to the amber
of a dream slowly sieved through sleep like a cloud—
you, in another body,
sometimes another planet.
Who could you have been
if the people before you had been someone else?
A doppelganger isn't so much a feat of human genetics
as a momentary glimpse
of the life you could have had.

Plate Tectonics

Continental drift, or, your present self
shifts relative to your past self
& your future self passes through you.
If mantle convection works as it should,
nostalgia also applies
to the worst years of your life,
sometimes, improbably, disguised as love.
Nothing moves without melting.
In other words, that blue house of your childhood
still stands, subterranean, in memory.
Beside it, the train tracks
where a woman screamed one night,
& the next morning there was a body.
That's the thing—maybe it was her,
but it could have been anyone.
You step into one life
& it either moves with you
or against you.

A Group of Grows Is Called a Murder

In Missouri, a suicide cluster so dense
it rivaled the stars.
One falling & another fallen.
All in college, only some in love—
sometimes, mystery looks almost
like understanding.
The way you grow up
is carrying your darkness through enough years
that it finally reaches the light.
When you stand at the edge of knowing
your life is finite,
it opens like a hand.
There are people who leave us every day
& only their shadows return.
Maybe that's why water ripples outward
after it's been touched—
a room can't be empty
when the room itself is inside it.
The doe always follows the lamb.

The Doppler Effect

Widely known in true crime spaces is the case of Maura Murray, who disappeared in New Hampshire in 2004 after a car crash and has not been found since.

All winter long, animals lie sleepless in their burrows.
An early frost, whales the size of houses
tangled in the reeds like stars.
Sometimes, a cell phone's last recorded ping
seeps out across the highway like oil.
Sometimes, a red light glowing in a car
against a snowbank
can be mistaken for a hawk.
Not communicating anything
to the other birds,
not returning a call home,
just watching.
If you have no idea where you're going,
you can't say where you've been.
In certain waters,
when a whale sings,
its echo lasts for miles.

The Final Girl

Is a horror movie trope referring to the last girl or woman alive to confront the killer.

A chair against the door
can either keep love in
or fear out.
Not every moon has jaws
& not every doe swerves back.
If you're the last one alive,
you're the first to understand.
Not how, but why.
It could be anything.
It could be a Wednesday.
And the dirt, red like ash.
Red like a stencil against Mars,
red like what flashes before your eyes.
Red like a woman's best color.
If you're what's left,
you're what's missing.

III. Memory

Ode to Petrichor

As a child, you lived with shadows,
pressed to the wall like a necklace.
At first light, the dawn would break & then the morning's milk,
white essence of a feather giving itself up to wind;
do you remember, now, how you believed there were rain dances
that could split the sky
& then suture & then split & then suture,
how every storm coincided with your body's new ache?
Growing up, there was that one friend
who ended his life before his life could end him,
but there was also the neighbor girl
who would pin her hair to her neck til it fell
like a blood clot through the eaves of her back,
how her barrette,
for one small moment, shone through the dark like a star.
That was childhood, then,
an insect passing through the amber of its tempered life,
and whole years still left ahead of you to forget.

Post-Apocalypse

All roads lead back to the same maple—
spectral, sweeping orange across the backyard pool.
When you left,
you left twice—
once from home, then from the hands that built it.
There were whole powerlines felled,
windshields splayed over the road like stars,
the world never any longer
than the width of our imagination.
If you're the last one standing,
you're the first to go.
Not because whatever's coming after this
is worse than what's already gone,
but because time can last longer
than you need it to,
like that one remaining tree
rehearsing its shadows like lines.

Elegy to Quarter-Life Crisis

When a tree falls in a forest, the resulting gap
leads to an explosion of butterflies.
Imagine,
killing a thing that gives life as it lays dying.
Like suiciding that part of yourself that always needs
to be in control, or watching a child twist the wings
off cicadas, not out of malice
but rather out of love, as if halting flight
is a favor to the sky they drown in.
You could be anything
& still you choose to be this.
Your adolescence of fables, your unmaking of beds
or—perhaps—entering the wrong ones.
Imagine, one day, all your years stretched out before you
like an abacus,
& the worst thing someone has ever done to you
crawls quietly in its cage like an insect,
body riddled with pink.

Dissertation on Nostalgia

In every shadowbox of your childhood,
another box for all the words you couldn't say.
Memory a chasm filled with snow.
Ambitious, to believe in color theory—
that you could combine the best parts with the worst
& produce something that won't haunt you.
Everyone has that singular moment
the world stopped,
for mere seconds or a second more,
when it was love at first sight
or regret at last glance.
What you remember poorly,
remembers you well.
And still the years ambered along like beads,
what you lost & gave
disappearing through the eye of a dream,
the desire to begin again, & again, & again
passing through each decade in verdant green.

The New Year

If measured, a decade spans a continent—
enduring, unspeakable,
the same way breath matches the curvature of loss.
Back then, you could pass through your childhood
like a knife, and the sun in the garden
was the first sun you'd ever seen,
somehow the last too,
even after every sun in all the years in between.
You were young, then,
so you could pour a double round of loss
& still reserve room for more,
the same way nothing can compare
to your first taste of language.
Not even stepping into a new body,
one horizon behind you,
the other in front,
blueness edged by the long winds of time.

Climate Change

In short, the first tree you ever climbed
is the last to emerge from your childhood.
The worst truths are the ones without reprieve,
no ladder long enough to touch,
& hardly any fruit to bear.
If you conclude the world is dying,
you also have to conclude
that someone put it there.
A salmon can swim upstream for days,
pink, jeweled like a lamp,
tossing in its own fevered dream,
& still end up miles from the coast.
Most perish after giving birth.
Imagine, loving something into a world
that doesn't love you back.
Things weren't better back then,
they just died a little slower.

Aesop's Fables

The Dog & the Oyster and The Eagle & the Jackdaw are two of his best-known works.

When the jackdaw saw the eagle carry away the lamb
& tried to replicate the killing,
the shepherd clipped its wings.
What comes first—the vanity or the vanishing?
Translated twice, this means—sometimes the past,
looking back, seems better than the past really was.
The sun was different then.
Molten, affixed to the sky like a pendant.
Even the dog swallowed the oyster whole,
drawn to its silver.
Not everything is worth the weight of loneliness
on the way down.
It wasn't the sunlight that changed, back then,
or the angle—
it was the viewer.
Everything seems glowing
when you remember it later.
Not just the pearl,
but even the scissors.

The Patron Saint of Leaving the Past in the Past

Everything in its right place.
Or, where you know you could find it again,
back to the childhood of bees,
winter of crows.
When the light dappled like marmalade
against the glass.
When there were still wedding rings
buried in the dirt.
When men didn't have hammers for their wives.
You could be seen, & not heard,
back then.
Now, you can't have either,
no iris raised from the dirt,
no fruit on the table
when you get home from school.
If you don't remember,
it didn't happen.
Not every trait
passes on.

IV. Melancholia

Theories of Loneliness

Petrichor is only beloved for its amnesiac properties—
you see rain, you think storm.
You see land, you think how much time remains.
Not until it gets better, whatever this is,
but until your life spills like a window
funneled into the basin of the ground.
If it were easy to be alone,
you'd be good at it by now.
If you count the seconds
between lightning & thunder,
a pattern emerges—
you've spent too much of your life
waiting for the next second of your life.
On some beaches, the carcass of a whale
rises far over the sand.
The bones could be a house, or a cell,
or a ship managed by a child's imagination.
That's the thing about loneliness—
sometimes, you can almost convince yourself
it's not exactly what it is.

Ode to the Worst Day of Your Life

You either taught me well, or taught me worse;
most days it's hard to decipher which.
You were the lion in the mouth of the lion.
You were the thing
that ate what ate what couldn't get away.
Once, a line of timbers burned for days
along the coast until emerging,
without warning, unscathed.
There was never any reason for their immolation—
no line of nefarious wolves, no curious hikers,
no identifiable spark.
You were the cause of every unimagined fire.
You, with your smoke like a shroud.
I carried every year of your grief on my back.
Not like a mother and child,
not like crossing a desert,
but tender,
like a lion who sees another lion
& knows there's only room for one.

Twelve Steps

Always the poem, even if nothing else.
The deer clustered like stars in the brush.
At least what's afraid of you
also sees you.
There are so many ways the world still turns—
burrs against your hair like an embrace,
another day without your name
in the obituaries,
a woman's joy so abundant
it misreads as hysteria.
Knowing that sadness, too, is a feeling;
it just feels a little worse.
When the sky opens like a hand,
somewhere else,
a person's heart is closing.
You have decades left
& decades after that.

Metonymy

The winter the neighbor explained to her child
that a seven-story building refers to the number of floors
and not, in fact, to a unique book assigned to each one,
you forgot how to color between the lines,
how to melody a piano, how to insert a window
in the rest of your life
& move, quietly, through the glass.
Sometimes, what hurt the most was a comb through your hair,
or a woman in the next stall with her back bent,
heaving, & the small, startling ineptitude
of your ability to save her.
Sometimes, what hurt the most
was your childhood phone number lost to memory,
its digits swimming darkly through the depths.
But there was a blood moon, once, pinned to the sky
like an iris, & the thought of an apartment building
filled with books, & the silver dollars dredged from the culvert
while your brother built a fort made of branches,
and sometimes, just for a while,
that was enough.

V. Milestones

Something Borrowed, Something Blue

As a child, you believed lakes
were poured into their final resting places
in the same shape they currently are,
water molded like clay to meet clay.
When a bear hibernated
it had just gone to its room.
When a whale washed up on the beach
it was just resting for a while.
When the marriage ended
it was just taking a break
til it could come back together again.
There were lakes that were bigger than others,
& some that were redder.
All of them structured by the same hand.
And the threshold between together & not
was so thin
it could have been a map.
Some things just aren't built
to accommodate everything inside them.

Lessons on Preparing for an Ending

Echinopsis, the Easter lily cactus,
blooms one night & withers the next.
It's not always so easy,
our rush to abundance.
At the center of your cellar lies enough
canning shelves to preserve an orchard.
You pickle, you brine, you oil & salt.
What you keep, becomes,
or it spreads.
If posed another way, the question
is how the diorama of your past house
holds up to your current house—
not just the windows, but mostly the bedroom.
Is it safe?
Have you winnowed the darkness?
What opens one night & leaves the next
still matters just as much as anything else
that was here your whole life.

Love Poem to Early Twenties

If the body works as intended,
it turns in sleep like color,
everything in its right place.
Curls down to your knees,
parted in the center—
Moses drawing back the Red Sea,
darkness of your childhood
fleeing like a storm.
You could do anything,
be anything, even,
and the world was verdant like a flood.
No rules, and more lives than a cat—
anything you wanted and then some,
and then almost too much,
years so far ahead
you could barely see them.

Thanatophobia

Every once in awhile, the phrase *stark raving mad*
comes to mind, as if your sanity is lost first
and then goes partying. As if anyone ever has any idea
what's in store for us, as if every slow pulse of existence
isn't perfectly calculated
to ruin love & then rebuild it.
Standing against a red window, an aneurysm could bloom
in your body like a tulip, or an arrhythmia
unfold like a cocktail,
something deep within you raised to the surface, at last,
burning.
This, here, is our undoing—
not enough reasons to stay
and not enough to leave.
And still nothing but life could keep you away from life,
could un-awe you from its cobalt thrill,
its endless memories folded like cut stems,
or the pure relief of hearing your own breath in the morning,
gratitude rising like a spill of fire.

Folie à Deux

*Folie à deux, or madness for two in French, refers to
a shared psychiatric disorder passed from one person to another.*

Understand this—most animals can do little better
than they already are.
At night, the syrup is tapped from the maples like stars,
salt piled at the ground like scales.
The worst thing one bear can do to another
is transform into a human.
Understand this—most stories passed down
are altered to save the listener.
The story of the owl left for dead
on the village doorstep,
the story of the lily so quietly held
against the window, body still pooling in rain.
Listen—your greatest fear, if told backwards,
looks almost like love.

Chrysalis

So many years later, the undoing of a relationship still lingers—
an almost-cradle, an almost-grave;
strange, how we begin & end
in the same shape.
The same multiphasic composure of stars.
In a parallel universe, you sleep on the ceiling
& walk over doors & there are birds for miles upon miles,
as far as the eye can see
& what happened is something that happened to someone else
in another time,
before the nurse asked whether you were ever violent
as the moon rose in the room like wine.
That winter, the olives hung rank on the tree
and there was nothing left to say,
nothing to say to make it right, nothing to do
to make it undo, just the onward march of the water
over the basin, the morels in their foothills,
and the almost unbearable knowledge
of a line quietly crossed.
That winter, I remember you one evening,
turning, to say
We do not love people; we only love who we think they are.
And the mountains ascended in the dark like ash,
the moment pouring into the next
before its resonance finally settled.

Non-Sonnet for Women Who Don't Want to Be Mothers

Once, a child's abacus took your breath away—
bead of loss, bead of undoing, bead of waking
in the morning & forgetting, for one brief moment,
your century of knives.
But how do you split a second, or carve the tongue
from a bell, or not pass down your absence of serotonin
to someone whose hand is so small
it could hold only one pill?
Sometimes, the sight of a school pressed against the dusk
thrills you like a chord, like rain
taking notes on sun, like desire growing deep like a molehill.
But then it ends—as things tend to do—
& the thought of carrying the responsibility of a future
is like your slow descent through the birth canal
so many years ago,
when, for one brief moment,
it was safer just to stay where you were.

Living Will

Nothing personal, mortality,
just light passing through an unanswered door.
How many different ways to spell moving on—
six feet under, kicked the bucket, bought the farm.
A colloquialism for a colloquialism
is what makes the worst things easier to say.
Or, ad infinitum—what you lose,
you lose again and again, forever.
A child will ask, with the patience of a child,
are we there yet?
The answer is yes,
or rather we thought we were,
the same way bought the farm really means
beneath the farm, the same way everything that matters
is just a euphemism for something else.
Not easy, to explain how life ends,
not easy, to carry the dust.
Someone has to plow what's left behind,
or be the thing that does the leaving.
In other words, if you get there first,
I'll join you later.

About the Author

Meggie Royer is a Midwest artist and writer working in the gender-based violence field. As a teen writer, she won a National Gold Medal for Poetry and Silver Medal for Writing Portfolio in the 2013 Scholastic Art & Writing Awards, and her artwork has been exhibited at the Octagon Center for the Arts in Iowa. Her most recent exhibit was a collection of mixed-media images displayed at the 17th Annual University of Michigan Sexual Assault Prevention and Awareness Center art show in April 2022.

Royer is the Founder and Editor-in-Chief of *Persephone's Daughters,* a literary and arts journal for abuse survivors. She has been nominated several times for the Pushcart Prize and was a finalist for the 2019 Princemere Poetry Prize. Royer's poetry has been published in *Plain China: National Anthology of the Best Undergraduate Writing, The Rumpus, The Minnesota Review, Tinderbox Poetry Journal,* and more.

She holds a Bachelor of Arts degree in Psychology from Macalester College and a Master of Social Work degree from the University of Michigan-Ann Arbor.

www.ingramcontent.com/pod-product-compliance
Lightning Source LLC
Chambersburg PA
CBHW030915170426
43193CB00009BA/852